CHAPTER

Being Compliant with HIPAA

A Comprehensive Guide

Wilder Angarita

How will this book reshape your understanding of HIPAA?

Engaging with "Being Compliant with HIPAA: A Comprehensive Guide" is more than just reading a book—it's embarking on a transformative journey. It's about evolving your understanding, fostering a culture of respect for patient privacy, and elevating the standards of your organization or practice.

1. **Comprehensive Understanding**: This guide is not just a rundown of do's and don'ts—it's a deep dive into HIPAA's essence. It fosters a complete understanding of the legislation's nuances and intricacies, allowing you to grasp not just the 'what,' but the 'why' behind each regulation.

2. **Empowerment Through Knowledge**: Knowledge is power, and in-depth understanding of HIPAA can empower you and your organization. It enables you to take proactive measures, anticipate potential pitfalls, and create an environment that respects privacy and security.

3. **Step-by-Step Guidance**: The guide is designed to lead you step by step through the process of building a HIPAA compliance program, simplifying complex procedures, and making the journey less daunting.

4. **Risk Management**: It provides valuable insights on risk assessment and management—a key aspect of HIPAA compliance. With these skills, you can identify

vulnerabilities and address them before they escalate into serious breaches.

5. **Future-Proof Your Compliance**: With a specific focus on HIPAA in the digital age, the guide helps future-proof your compliance efforts. It offers guidance on dealing with emerging technologies, telehealth, and mobile apps, preparing you for the landscape of tomorrow.

6. **Cultivating a Culture of Compliance**: The guide emphasizes the importance of developing a culture of compliance within your organization. This culture goes beyond mere rule-following—it promotes a deep-seated respect for patient privacy and a commitment to upholding the highest standards of data security.

7. **Become an Authority**: Reading this guide will set you apart as an authority on HIPAA compliance in your organization. You'll be a go-to resource for your colleagues, enhancing your professional value.

8. **Avoiding Penalties**: Non-compliance can result in severe penalties. This guide helps you avoid such repercussions by ensuring that you're fully informed about HIPAA's requirements.

Reading "Being Compliant with HIPAA: A Comprehensive Guide" is an investment that pays rich dividends. It's an investment in knowledge, in your organization, in your career, and, most importantly, in the trust and wellbeing of the patients you serve. This guide isn't just about being compliant—it's about being exceptional in the healthcare industry.

So, let's embark on this journey together. Let's learn, understand, and innovate. For in the heart of compliance, we find better care, better services, and a better healthcare community. Welcome to "Being Compliant with HIPAA: A Comprehensive Guide." It's time to turn the page and begin.

Table of Contents

CHAPTER 1

Introduction to HIPAA

Welcome to "Being Compliant with HIPAA: A Comprehensive Guide." In this chapter, we will embark on a journey through the history, purpose, and significance of the Health Insurance Portability and Accountability Act (HIPAA). With the increasing digitization of health information and the growing threats to privacy, understanding and complying with HIPAA has never been more critical.

Imagine a world where your most sensitive health information could be easily accessed, stolen, or even sold without your knowledge. Frightening, isn't it? This was the reality for many individuals before HIPAA came into existence. In 1996, the U.S. Congress enacted HIPAA to address the widespread concerns about the privacy and security of patients' health information. Since then, it has become a cornerstone of the healthcare system, guiding healthcare providers, insurers, and other organizations in handling patients' data with the utmost care and responsibility.

HIPAA serves several key purposes. First, it aims to protect patients' health information, ensuring that their privacy is respected and safeguarded. Second, it establishes standards and guidelines for the secure handling, storage, and transmission of electronic health information. Third, it intends to streamline the administration of health insurance by reducing fraud, waste, and abuse in the system.

Who is affected by HIPAA? The answer is virtually everyone involved in the healthcare industry. The law applies to a wide range of organizations and individuals, including healthcare providers, health plans, healthcare clearinghouses, and even the business associates who work with these organizations. Essentially, if you handle patients' health information in any capacity, HIPAA matters to you.

While understanding and implementing HIPAA may seem like a daunting task, it is essential for maintaining patients' trust and preserving the integrity of the healthcare system. In this book, I will break down the complex world of HIPAA into manageable, digestible pieces. Each chapter will focus on a different aspect of HIPAA, guiding you through the rules, requirements, and best practices for compliance.

As you read this book, you will gain valuable insights into the workings of HIPAA and learn how to build a robust compliance program for your organization. In the end, you'll be better equipped to navigate the challenges of protecting patients' health information and ensuring the security of electronic health records.

As we proceed through this chapter, let's delve a bit deeper into the context that gave rise to HIPAA. The late 20th century saw the rapid expansion of computer technology and the internet, revolutionizing the way we store, process, and share information. The healthcare industry was not immune to these changes. In fact, the adoption of electronic health records (EHRs) and other digital systems brought about numerous benefits, such as improved patient care, more efficient billing processes, and enhanced communication between providers.

However, this digital transformation also exposed vulnerabilities. Healthcare organizations grapple with the challenges of keeping sensitive patient information secure in an increasingly interconnected world. Incidents of medical identity theft and unauthorized access to health records became all too common, eroding public trust in the healthcare system.

Recognizing these challenges, Congress took action by passing HIPAA. The law was designed to strike a delicate balance between promoting the efficient use of technology in healthcare and ensuring the privacy and security of patients' health information. To achieve this, HIPAA provides a set of uniform standards that organizations must adhere to when handling health data. It also empowers patients with rights and control over their own health information.

Throughout this book, you will encounter real-life examples and case studies that showcase the importance of HIPAA compliance. These stories will not only emphasize the consequences of noncompliance but also highlight the positive impact that HIPAA has had on patients and the healthcare system as a whole. By understanding the practical implications of HIPAA, you will be better prepared to make informed decisions and implement effective strategies for your organization.

As we embark on this journey to explore the intricacies of HIPAA, it is crucial to remember that compliance is not just about meeting legal requirements. It is also about fostering a culture of privacy and security within your organization. This means that every member of your team, from the frontline staff to the executive leadership, must understand the value of protecting patients' health information and take an active role in maintaining compliance.

With the right mindset and commitment to continuous improvement, HIPAA compliance becomes not just an obligation, but an opportunity – an opportunity to build trust with patients, streamline operations, and ultimately provide better care.

So, let's take this first step together toward a deeper understanding of HIPAA and its significance in the ever-evolving world of healthcare.

2

Understanding HIPAA Regulations

As we delve deeper into this chapter, let's view HIPAA regulations not as burdensome hurdles to overcome, but as essential building blocks in crafting a secure and privacy-focused healthcare environment.

To thoroughly grasp the Privacy Rule, imagine you're a librarian of a unique library, where the books are patients' health records. These records, like rare books, are highly valuable and sensitive, and it's your job to ensure they're not misused or shared without the proper permission. This rule outlines the instances where PHI can be used or disclosed and emphasizes the principle of 'minimum necessary'—a concept that encourages using or sharing only the necessary amount of PHI required to accomplish a task.

Moving on to the Security Rule, visualize that you're now the architect, tasked with designing a fortress to protect this unique library. You need to consider the administrative aspects (policies and procedures), the physical measures (like locks and surveillance systems), and technical safeguards (like firewalls and encryption). The Security Rule is all about crafting this fortress with layered defenses to protect electronic health information from a variety of threats.

The Breach Notification Rule comes into play when there's a breach in the fortress. If a thief manages to infiltrate and steal a book, what should you do? This rule lays out the necessary steps for notifying the appropriate parties in the aftermath of a breach. It underscores the importance of transparency and responsibility in maintaining the public's trust.

Lastly, the Enforcement Rule functions as the governing council overseeing this unique library. If you fail in your responsibilities, this council will hold you accountable. Penalties vary based on the nature and extent of the violation, and whether reasonable efforts were made to correct the violation. This rule underscores that HIPAA is not merely a suggestion, but a law with real-world consequences for non-compliance.

Remember, HIPAA regulations aren't just about compliance— they're about respecting the privacy and rights of patients. It's about fostering a culture where every member of the team understands the importance of protecting health information.

Let's review the 4 rules one more time with a different set of examples:

The Privacy Rule is all about respecting and safeguarding Protected Health Information (PHI). Let's take the case of a hospital nurse, Sarah. One day, her neighbor asks about the health of a mutual friend who's been admitted to Sarah's hospital. Even if Sarah knows the details, the Privacy Rule mandates she mustn't disclose this information. The rule prioritizes patient confidentiality and restricts the sharing of PHI to scenarios of treatment, payment, or healthcare operations, or when the patient has provided explicit consent.

Moving onto the Security Rule, this regulation is about protecting Electronic PHI (ePHI) through three types of safeguards: administrative, physical, and technical. Consider a healthcare clinic upgrading its record-keeping from paper to digital. Under the Security Rule, the clinic would need administrative safeguards like relevant policies and procedures, training programs for staff, and contingency plans for emergencies. Physical safeguards could involve secure workstations, locking mechanisms for devices, and proper device disposal methods. Technical safeguards might include unique user identification for system access, encryption and decryption of ePHI, and regular audit logs and trails.

Next, the Breach Notification Rule comes into play when there's a breach of unsecured PHI. Suppose a laptop containing unencrypted ePHI gets stolen from a physician's car. The physician's practice must first assess the breach's harm level. If there's a significant risk, they must notify affected individuals without unreasonable delay, but no later than 60 days. For breaches involving over 500 residents of a state or jurisdiction, media outlets must also be informed. Additionally, all breaches must be reported to the HHS, with larger breaches being reported sooner.

Lastly, the Enforcement Rule deals with the repercussions of HIPAA non-compliance. For instance, a pharmacy chain once disposed of documents containing patient information in an unsecured dumpster. Following an HHS investigation, the pharmacy chain had to pay a fine of $2.25 million due to their improper PHI disposal practices. This example illustrates how the Enforcement Rule ensures accountability and adherence to HIPAA.

Each of these rules intertwines, creating a robust framework for the protection of patient health information. By understanding the specifics of each rule and the interplay between them, you can ensure a more effective, holistic approach to HIPAA compliance.

As we continue our journey through HIPAA's complex landscape, remember that these rules serve as our compass, guiding us towards responsible and ethical handling of health information. By fully understanding and applying these rules, we contribute to a safer, more trustworthy healthcare environment for all.

3

Key Terms and Definitions

Chapter 3: Key Terms and Definitions, is an exploration of these critical elements: Covered Entities, Business Associates, Protected Health Information (PHI), and Electronic Protected Health Information (ePHI). These terms form the foundation of HIPAA, and a comprehensive understanding of them is paramount for any healthcare organization seeking to achieve and maintain compliance.

Covered Entities

The first of these essential threads is 'Covered Entities'. The term refers to the types of organizations and individuals that are directly subject to HIPAA regulations. These primarily include health plans, health care clearinghouses, and health care providers that transmit health information in electronic form for transactions for which the Secretary of Health and Human Services has adopted standards under HIPAA. Each of these categories encompasses a broad range of entities. For instance, health plans include health insurance companies, company health plans, government programs that pay for healthcare, and others.

Business Associates

Next, we come to 'Business Associates.' Business associates are individuals or entities that perform services for, or on behalf of, a covered entity that involves the use or disclosure of protected health information (PHI). The scope of 'business associates' can be broad, including third-party administrators, an IT provider handling PHI, or even a lawyer provided with PHI for legal services. Importantly, business associates are also directly subject to many HIPAA rules and must ensure they have safeguards in place to protect the PHI they handle.

Protected Health Information (PHI)

Protected Health Information, commonly referred to as PHI, forms the heart of HIPAA. PHI is any information that is held by a covered entity or its business associates, which concerns health status, provision of health care, or payment for health care that can be linked to an individual. This is interpreted rather broadly and includes any part of an individual's medical record or payment history. PHI could range from medical diagnoses to payment receipts for medical services, and even appointment schedules.

Electronic Protected Health Information (ePHI)

Finally, Electronic Protected Health Information or ePHI. As technology has permeated healthcare, it has given rise to a new category of PHI, which is transmitted or maintained in any electronic medium. ePHI is subject to the same protections as PHI but also has additional security rules to address the unique vulnerabilities associated with electronic data. These rules address technical and non-technical safeguards, such as access controls,

audit controls, transmission security, and device and media controls.

Understanding these key terms and definitions is similar to mastering the alphabet of HIPAA. These terms represent the core concepts around which the rest of the regulations revolve. As we delve deeper into the nuances of HIPAA compliance, these foundational concepts will repeatedly come into play, guiding the implementation of policies and procedures. The path to HIPAA compliance begins with a firm grasp of these fundamental terms, setting the stage for a comprehensive understanding of the law in its entirety.

4

Building Your HIPAA Compliance Program

Welcome to Chapter 4, where we will take the knowledge we've gained so far and begin to apply it in a practical, real-world context. It's time to roll up our sleeves and get into the process of building your HIPAA compliance program. This chapter is akin to a master class in crafting a bespoke suit, where HIPAA is the fabric, your organization is the wearer, and the compliance program is the well-tailored suit that fits just right.

In building a HIPAA compliance program, it's crucial to remember that this isn't a one-size-fits-all situation. Every healthcare entity has unique needs and circumstances, which means your compliance program should be tailored to fit your organization perfectly.

Developing policies and procedures

Policies and procedures act as the roadmap to HIPAA compliance for any healthcare organization. They outline the expectations, behaviors, and actions required to safeguard Protected Health Information (PHI) and Electronic Protected Health Information (ePHI). Policies are high-level guidelines that express the organization's commitment to comply with the requirements of HIPAA. Procedures, on the other hand, are detailed, step-by-step instructions that provide a clear course of action for fulfilling these policies.

Developing policies and procedures is not a one-size-fits-all process. It must be tailored to fit the size, complexity, and nature of the specific healthcare organization. The policies and procedures should take into account the scope of the organization's operations, the types of PHI it handles, and the potential risks to that information. They should be broad enough to cover all potential scenarios but specific enough to provide clear guidance.

The development process begins with a thorough understanding of the HIPAA regulations and the organization's obligations under the law. These obligations should then be translated into specific policies. For instance, a policy could state that the organization will restrict access to PHI to only those employees who need it to perform their job functions.

Once the policies are established, procedures should be developed to implement them. Using our earlier example, a procedure could outline the process for determining which job roles require access to PHI, how access is granted, and how it is revoked when no longer needed.

It's essential that the policies and procedures are documented and easily accessible to all staff. This not only helps in training and compliance but also demonstrates to regulators that the organization has a strong commitment to HIPAA compliance.

Keep in mind that policies and procedures are not static documents. They should be reviewed regularly and updated as necessary to reflect changes in the organization, technology, or the regulatory environment.

With well-crafted policies and procedures, an organization arms itself with the necessary tools to navigate the complex landscape of HIPAA regulations. This critical first step in building a HIPAA Compliance Program is the cornerstone of sustained compliance, providing a solid foundation from which the organization can confidently move forward.

Let's review an example of a PHI Management and Breach Response Policy:

Protected Health Information (PHI) Management and Breach Response Policy

1. *Purpose*
   The purpose of this policy is to establish guidelines for managing and protecting Protected Health Information (PHI), as required by the Health Insurance Portability and Accountability Act (HIPAA). This policy outlines procedures for using and disclosing PHI, respecting individuals' rights, responding to data breaches, and enforcing disciplinary actions for violations.

2. *Scope*
   This policy applies to all employees, contractors, volunteers, and third parties who have access to, or are responsible for, handling PHI within the organization.

3. *Definitions*
   3.1. PHI: Protected Health Information refers to any information that can be used to identify an individual and is related to their health condition, healthcare provision, or payment for healthcare.

4. *Use and Disclosure of PHI*
   4.1. The organization will use and disclose PHI only as necessary for treatment, payment, and healthcare operations unless otherwise authorized by the individual or as required by law.

   4.2. Any disclosures of PHI must be done on a minimum necessary basis, sharing only the information required for the purpose.

5. *Rights of Individuals*
   5.1. Individuals have the right to request access to their PHI, request corrections or amendments, and receive an accounting of disclosures.

   5.2. Requests must be handled in a timely manner, as per the established procedures of the organization.

6. *Data Breach Response*
   6.1. The organization has a defined process for identifying, responding to, and reporting data breaches involving PHI.

   6.2. Affected individuals, the Department of Health and Human Services, and, in some cases, the media must be notified of breaches as required by law.

7. *Disciplinary Actions*
   7.1. Violations of this policy may result in disciplinary action, up to and including termination of employment or contract.

   7.2. Violations may also result in civil and criminal penalties under HIPAA.

8. *Roles and Responsibilities*
   8.1. The HIPAA Compliance Officer is responsible for the implementation and enforcement of this policy.

   8.2. All personnel are responsible for complying with this policy and reporting any suspected or confirmed violations or breaches.

9. *Policy Review and Update*
   9.1. This policy will be reviewed and updated at least annually, or when significant changes occur within the organization, to ensure it continues to meet the organization's needs and legal obligations.

By adhering to this policy, the organization aims to ensure the privacy and security of PHI, while maintaining the highest level of service and care for our patients.

Now, I want you to keep in mind that policies normally are high-level documents, if you want to create a document that details the who, how, what, when and why, then you need to create a procedure, which is more appropriate for this type of situations and provides that level of granularity.

Risk assessment and management

Risk assessment is the act of identifying potential threats and vulnerabilities that could compromise the integrity of Protected Health Information (PHI) and Electronic Protected Health Information (ePHI). It is a proactive approach, a means to anticipate and mitigate potential breaches before they occur. The intention is not to eliminate all risks (an impossible feat), but rather to reduce risk to a reasonable and appropriate level in accordance with the organization's risk tolerance.

The risk assessment process comprises several key steps. Firstly, the scope of the assessment needs to be identified. This includes determining the systems, processes, and locations where PHI and ePHI are stored, transmitted, or processed. Once the scope is set, potential threats and vulnerabilities to these assets should be identified. A threat could be anything that has the potential to cause harm, such as a cyber attack or a natural disaster, while a vulnerability is a weakness that could be exploited by a threat.

After the threats and vulnerabilities are identified, their potential impact and the likelihood of their occurrence are evaluated. The combination of these two factors determines the level of risk. A high-impact, high-likelihood scenario would be considered a high risk, while a low-impact, low-likelihood scenario would be considered a low risk.

The culmination of the risk assessment is a risk report, a comprehensive document that details the identified risks, their potential impact, and the controls that are currently in place to mitigate them. It is from this report that the risk management plan is born.

Risk management is the response to the risk assessment. It is the process of deciding what actions to take in response to identified risks. This could involve mitigating the risk by implementing additional security measures, transferring the risk through insurance, accepting the risk if it is within the organization's risk tolerance, or avoiding the risk entirely by changing business processes.

The risk management plan should also include regular monitoring and review of the identified risks and the effectiveness of the controls in place. Risks can change over time, as can an organization's ability to manage them. Regular reassessment ensures that the organization stays ahead of the game, continually updating and adjusting its risk management strategy in response to evolving circumstances.

Understanding and effectively implementing risk assessment and management is paramount to maintaining HIPAA compliance. This dynamic process forms the backbone of an effective HIPAA Compliance Program, fostering a culture of vigilance and proactive response that is critical in the ever-evolving landscape of healthcare data security.

Workforce training and awareness

Now we step into an arena where knowledge is power, and ignorance is a potent risk - workforce training and awareness. A robust HIPAA compliance program requires more than policies, procedures, and risk assessments; it is significantly reliant on the understanding and cooperation of the individuals who handle Protected Health Information (PHI) on a daily basis.

Workforce training is a foundational pillar of any HIPAA Compliance Program. It is not merely an optional extra, but a regulatory requirement under the HIPAA Privacy and Security Rules. Every member of the workforce, including employees, volunteers, trainees, and even contractors, who have access to PHI, must undergo training to ensure they understand the HIPAA rules and the organization's specific policies and procedures related to PHI. This applies to all levels of the organization, from executive management down to the newest recruit.

The training program should be tailored to the needs of the organization and the role of the individual. For example, staff members involved in billing may need specific instruction on how to handle billing information in a HIPAA-compliant manner, while IT personnel may require training on safeguarding ePHI against cyber threats. Despite the individualized nature of the content, all training should cover the basics of HIPAA, including an overview of the Privacy, Security, and Breach Notification Rules, as well as the rights of individuals under HIPAA.

But training should not be a one-time event. It should be ongoing and iterative, evolving as the regulations, technology, and organizational practices change. Refresher courses should be periodically provided to keep the workforce up-to-date and to reinforce the importance of HIPAA compliance. Furthermore, additional training should be provided whenever there is a material change in the law or the organization's policies and procedures.

Beyond formal training, fostering an environment of awareness is equally critical. This involves creating a culture where privacy and security are valued and respected. Regular reminders, bulletins, and updates about HIPAA issues can be helpful tools in maintaining this awareness. Also, fostering open communication where employees feel comfortable asking questions or reporting potential issues is crucial in maintaining an environment of compliance.

In summary, workforce training and awareness is a multifaceted endeavor. It is an exercise in education, communication, and culture building. It is also a journey rather than a destination, a continuous process of learning and adaptation. With the right approach, organizations can transform their workforce into their strongest line of defense in preserving the privacy and security of health information.

Designating a HIPAA Privacy and Security Officer

Stepping into the fourth section of Chapter 4, we begin to discuss the pivotal role of leadership in maintaining HIPAA compliance. One of the most crucial responsibilities within an organization's HIPAA compliance program is the designation of a HIPAA Privacy and Security Officer. This role isn't merely a suggestion, but a requirement outlined within the HIPAA Privacy and Security Rules.

The HIPAA Privacy Officer and the Security Officer may be the same person or two different people, depending on the size and complexity of the organization. In smaller practices, one person might manage both roles, whereas larger organizations may require separate individuals or even entire teams to manage the responsibilities of each role.

The HIPAA Privacy Officer is responsible for developing and implementing privacy policies and procedures. This role involves ensuring that the organization's practices align with federal and state privacy laws, particularly those related to the use and disclosure of PHI. The Privacy Officer also oversees the training of the workforce on these policies and procedures, handles privacy complaints, and coordinates with the Security Officer to mitigate any breaches of unsecured PHI.

On the other hand, the HIPAA Security Officer's role is focused on the protection of electronic PHI (ePHI). The Security Officer is responsible for creating and implementing policies and procedures to ensure the confidentiality, integrity, and availability of ePHI. This individual oversees risk assessments and risk management processes, ensuring that appropriate security measures are in place to protect ePHI against potential threats.

Both roles require excellent leadership, communication, and analytical skills. They also require a thorough understanding of the HIPAA regulations, along with the operational workings of the organization. Furthermore, both roles require collaboration with various departments within the organization, including IT, human resources, legal, and top management.

While the responsibilities of these roles are extensive, the importance of having dedicated individuals to oversee the organization's HIPAA compliance cannot be overstated. By designating a HIPAA Privacy and Security Officer, an organization ensures that there is an accountable party who is consistently monitoring the organization's privacy and security practices, thereby reducing the risk of non-compliance and potential penalties.

In this era where data breaches are becoming increasingly common, these roles serve as the organization's vanguard, ensuring the protection of valuable health information while fostering trust with patients and partners. These officers are not merely roles within the organization but critical components of the organization's commitment to safeguarding health information.

5

Ensuring Privacy of Health Information

Patient Rights Under HIPAA

As we embark on the first section of Chapter 5, we delve into the cornerstone of HIPAA: the rights it provides to patients concerning their health information. These rights are like a protective shield, enabling patients to exercise control over their personal health information (PHI). By understanding these rights, healthcare professionals can not only comply with the law but also foster trust and respect with their patients.

Firstly, patients have the right to access their PHI. This right empowers patients to view or obtain copies of their health records, whether they are stored electronically or on paper. It is crucial for healthcare providers to have a system in place for promptly responding to these requests, as failure to do so can lead to non-compliance.

Secondly, patients have the right to request amendments to their health records. If a patient believes that there is an error in their PHI or that important information is missing, they can request the healthcare provider to rectify it. It is important for healthcare providers to respond to these requests in a timely manner and to ensure their systems are equipped to handle such amendments.

Thirdly, HIPAA provides patients with the right to an accounting of disclosures. This right enables patients to find out when, to whom, and for what purpose their PHI has been disclosed. As a healthcare provider, it is essential to maintain accurate records of all disclosures of PHI to fulfil these requests when they arise.

Lastly, patients have the right to request restrictions on the use and disclosure of their PHI. Although healthcare providers are not always required to agree to these requests, it is important to have a system in place for considering and responding to them.

Use and Disclosure of PHI

In this new section of Chapter 5, we'll unravel the specifics of the use and disclosure of Protected Health Information (PHI). Navigating these guidelines is much like understanding the blueprints of a complex architectural design. Each detail serves a purpose, and when combined, they contribute to a well-structured, secure edifice of healthcare data protection.

PHI is the lifeblood of healthcare operations. It includes a vast array of information linked to an individual, ranging from medical records, treatment details, and billing information, to conversations between healthcare providers about a patient's care. Understanding how to use and disclose this information in compliance with HIPAA is vital for any healthcare entity.

The use of PHI within a healthcare organization refers to the internal sharing, application, utilization, examination, or analysis of such information. Disclosure, conversely, represents the external release, transfer, provision of access to, or divulging in any other manner of information outside the entity holding the information.

Under the HIPAA Privacy Rule, PHI can be used and disclosed without a patient's express consent for three central activities: treatment, payment, and healthcare operations.

Treatment: This involves the provision, coordination, or management of healthcare and related services among healthcare providers or by a healthcare provider with a third party, consultation between healthcare providers, and patient referrals.

Payment: Here, the focus is on activities that enable the provider to get reimbursed for the healthcare services they offer. This could include billing, claims management, eligibility determination, and utilization review.

Healthcare Operations: This broad category encompasses activities such as quality assessment and improvement, training, licensing, and conducting or arranging for medical reviews and audits.

In these instances, PHI flows seamlessly within and between healthcare entities, fueling the engine of healthcare delivery while staying within the HIPAA compliance boundaries.

However, for other activities such as research, marketing, or sale of PHI, HIPAA requires explicit patient authorization. This authorization should be detailed, highlighting who will disclose and receive the PHI, the purpose of the disclosure, and an expiration date for the authorization.

Gaining a deep understanding of the rules surrounding the use and disclosure of PHI is critical. It not only ensures HIPAA compliance but also fortifies the sacred bond of trust between healthcare providers and patients. When patients can confidently entrust their sensitive health information to their healthcare providers, knowing that it will be used judiciously and disclosed only when necessary, they can truly invest their trust in the healthcare system.

In the realm of HIPAA, every rule and regulation serves a higher purpose - preserving patient privacy and bolstering the integrity of our healthcare system. By the end of this section, you will have a robust understanding of the guidelines governing the use and disclosure of PHI, equipping you with the knowledge needed to safeguard patient information while rendering the best possible care.

As we move forward, I invite you to delve deeper into these guidelines, absorbing the knowledge and incorporating it into your daily operations. I'll leave you at this juncture, offering you the space to further explore this topic, fostering a culture of privacy and compliance within your healthcare organization.

Notice of Privacy Practices

As we turn the page to the next section of Chapter 5, we encounter the Notice of Privacy Practices, a fundamental instrument in the orchestra of HIPAA compliance. This document, much like a lighthouse, serves to guide patients through the complexities of how their PHI is used and disclosed, casting a beam of transparency into the often-opaque waters of healthcare information practices.

The Notice of Privacy Practices is a document that healthcare providers are required to develop and distribute to their patients. This notice should clearly state the ways in which the healthcare provider may use and disclose a patient's health information. It should also inform patients about their rights under HIPAA and how they can exercise these rights.

The Notice of Privacy Practices is not merely a formality. It is a critical tool for fostering open communication between healthcare providers and patients. By clearly explaining how patients' information is used, it helps build trust and confidence in the healthcare system.

There are several key components that must be included in the Notice of Privacy Practices:

How PHI May Be Used and Disclosed: The notice should detail the circumstances under which PHI may be used and disclosed, including for treatment, payment, and health care operations, and other purposes as required or permitted by law.

Individual Rights: The notice should clearly outline the patient's rights under HIPAA, including the right to access and amend their PHI, the right to an accounting of disclosures, and the right to request restrictions on certain uses and disclosures.

Healthcare Provider Duties: The notice should also include a statement of the healthcare provider's legal duties, such as the obligation to maintain the privacy of PHI and to provide individuals with a notice of its legal duties and privacy practices.

Complaints: The notice must inform individuals of their right to file a complaint with the healthcare provider or with the Secretary of Health and Human Services if they believe their privacy rights have been violated.

Contact Information: Lastly, the notice should provide the name, or title, and telephone number of the person or office to contact for further information about the healthcare provider's privacy practices.

Creating a comprehensive and understandable Notice of Privacy Practices is no small task, but it is a vital step in upholding the principles of HIPAA. By detailing your organization's practices and the rights of patients in a clear and accessible manner, you can foster a transparent and trusting relationship with the individuals you serve.

I invite you to take a moment to reflect on your own Notice of Privacy Practices. Does it accurately reflect your organization's practices? Does it clearly outline patient rights? Remember, the Notice of Privacy Practices is more than a document—it's a statement of your commitment to privacy and respect.

Authorization and Consent

Moving further into the depths of Chapter 5, we arrive at the pivotal topic of Authorization and Consent. This subject, in the context of HIPAA, is akin to a key that unlocks the doors to the use and disclosure of Protected Health Information (PHI). Understanding this key's design, its function, and when it should be used is essential for every healthcare provider striving for HIPAA compliance.

To begin, it's critical to distinguish between 'consent' and 'authorization' as they have specific meanings under HIPAA.

Consent refers to the agreement by a patient for a covered entity to use and disclose PHI for treatment, payment, or health care operations (TPO). Before the Privacy Rule modifications of 2013, obtaining such consent was a common practice, but it's no longer required. However, providers can still choose to obtain consent for TPO uses and disclosures, but they must adhere to the specific terms of that consent.

Authorization, on the other hand, is a more detailed agreement for the use and disclosure of PHI. It's required for uses and disclosures outside of TPO, with a few exceptions (such as when disclosure is required by law). An authorization must specify a number of elements, including a description of the PHI to be used and disclosed, the person(s) disclosing and receiving the PHI, an expiration date, and, in some cases, the purpose for the disclosure.

The Privacy Rule generally requires healthcare providers to obtain written authorization from patients before disclosing their PHI. However, it's not an absolute requirement; there are exceptions where PHI can be disclosed without an authorization, such as for public health activities, reporting victims of abuse, neglect, or domestic violence, and for law enforcement purposes.

Compliance with the authorization and consent requirements of HIPAA signifies a healthcare provider's commitment to maintaining the confidentiality and integrity of the patient's PHI. It is an essential aspect of building trust with patients, as it gives them control over who has access to their sensitive health information.

Stop for a second and reflect on the following questions: Are your authorization processes robust and compliant? Does your team understand when and how to obtain valid authorization? Reflecting on these questions can help ensure your practices align with HIPAA's commitment to privacy and transparency.

Securing Electronic Health Information

Administrative Safeguards

As we venture into Chapter 6, our attention turns towards securing Electronic Health Information (EHI). To start, we'll focus on the first layer of protection: Administrative Safeguards. These safeguards form the framework of a solid security management process, a bit like the foundation and supporting beams in a building, providing the necessary structure to prevent, detect, contain, and correct security violations.

The HIPAA Security Rule defines administrative safeguards as 'administrative actions, and policies and procedures, to manage the selection, development, implementation, and maintenance of security measures to protect electronic protected health information and to manage the conduct of the covered entity's workforce in relation to the protection of that information.' In simpler terms, they are the guidelines and procedures that help to manage and oversee the protection of EHI.

Administrative safeguards encompass a range of aspects, including:

Security Management Process: This involves identifying potential risks to the EHI and implementing security measures to lower those risks to an acceptable level. Regular risk analysis and risk management are key components of this process.

Security Personnel: A designated security officer should be responsible for developing and implementing security policies and procedures.

Information Access Management: This ensures that only authorized personnel have access to EHI. It includes implementing procedures for authorized access and modifying access when necessary, such as during personnel changes.

Workforce Training and Management: This involves training all workforce members on the security policies and procedures of the entity. It also includes applying appropriate sanctions against workforce members who violate these policies and procedures.

Evaluation: Regular evaluations of the security policies and procedures should be carried out to ensure they adequately protect EHI, particularly in response to environmental or operational changes affecting the security of EHI.

Contingency Plan: This plan prepares the entity to respond to emergencies that may damage systems containing EHI, including data backup plans, disaster recovery plans, and emergency mode operation plans.

The importance of administrative safeguards cannot be overstated. These safeguards form the backbone of a strong security system, creating a structure that supports all other security efforts. They help to build an organizational culture that prioritizes the protection of EHI, guiding employees' behavior and shaping their interactions with these sensitive data.

As you reflect on the administrative safeguards within your own organization, consider how they can be strengthened. Are they comprehensive? Do they cover all necessary areas? Are they regularly reviewed and updated? Your reflections on these questions will guide your ongoing journey towards robust HIPAA compliance.

Physical Safeguards

Physical safeguards are akin to the walls and doors of a building, providing tangible protection against unauthorized access to information. In the digital world, these safeguards act as a physical barrier, protecting electronic systems and the data they contain from physical threats and environmental hazards.

Under the HIPAA Security Rule, physical safeguards are defined as "physical measures, policies, and procedures to protect a covered entity's electronic information systems and related buildings and equipment, from natural and environmental hazards, and unauthorized intrusion."

These safeguards encompass four main areas:

Facility Access Controls: These are the measures put in place to limit physical access to facilities containing EHI while ensuring that authorized access is allowed. This could include access control and validation procedures, maintenance records, and contingency operations.

Workstation Use: Policies and procedures must specify the proper functions to be performed, the manner in which those functions are to be performed, and the physical attributes of the surroundings of a specific workstation or class of workstation that can access EHI.

Workstation Security: Physical safeguards are needed for all workstations that can access EHI, to restrict unauthorized users from accessing these workstations. This could be as simple as positioning screens in a way that passersby cannot see sensitive information, or it could involve more complex security measures.

Device and Media Controls: Policies and procedures that govern the receipt and removal of hardware and electronic media that contain EHI into and out of a facility, and the movement of these items within the facility, are essential. This includes disposal, media re-use, accountability, and data backup and storage.

In the era of digital health, we must remember that the protection of EHI is not solely about virtual barriers and digital firewalls. The physical security of the equipment and facilities housing this information is equally important.

As we continue our exploration of HIPAA safeguards, consider the physical barriers protecting your EHI. Are they robust? Do they cover all potential points of access? Regular assessments of these safeguards will ensure they continue to provide the strongest possible protection for your EHI.

Technical Safeguards

Continuing our journey through the terrain of EHI protection, we arrive at the third category of safeguards: Technical Safeguards. These are similar to the sophisticated alarm systems and digital locks of a building, providing an additional layer of protection that leverages technology to protect EHI and control access to it.

The HIPAA Security Rule defines technical safeguards as "the technology and the policy and procedures for its use that protect electronic protected health information and control access to it."

Technical safeguards encompass five main areas:

Access Control: This refers to the technical policies and procedures that allow only authorized persons to access electronic protected health information (e-PHI). It involves unique user identification, emergency access procedures, automatic logoff, and encryption and decryption.

For example, let's consider a hospital setting where a doctor needs to access the medical records of a patient. The doctor will have a unique user ID and password or other authentication methods (like a fingerprint or smart card) to access the EHI. In the event of an emergency, there should be procedures in place for the doctor to access this information quickly.

Audit Controls: These are the hardware, software, and procedural mechanisms that record and examine activity in information systems that contain or use e-PHI.

Let's use the example of a healthcare insurance company that needs to audit access to its customers' e-PHI. The company can use software that records when each record was accessed, who accessed it, and what changes were made. This helps in detecting any unauthorized access or anomalies.

Integrity Controls: This refers to the policies and procedures to ensure that e-PHI is not altered or destroyed in an unauthorized manner. It includes mechanisms to corroborate that e-PHI has not been altered or destroyed in an unauthorized manner.

For instance, imagine a research institution that stores sensitive health data for long-term studies. To maintain data integrity, the institution could employ checksum systems, where data blocks are assigned a unique identifier. If data is tampered with or corrupted, the identifier changes, signaling an integrity issue.

Authentication: Entities must implement procedures to verify that a person or entity seeking access to e-PHI is indeed who they claim to be.

Take an example of a telemedicine app where patients can consult with healthcare providers remotely. The app could use multi-factor authentication, such as requiring a password and a one-time code sent to the user's phone, to verify the identity of the user before granting access to e-PHI.

Transmission Security: This refers to the technical security measures that guard against unauthorized access to e-PHI being transmitted over a network.

Consider a pharmacist sending a prescription order to a drug wholesaler. To ensure transmission security, the pharmacist could use a Virtual Private Network (VPN), which encrypts the data, making it unreadable to anyone who might intercept the transmission.

Technical safeguards are integral to securing EHI. As technology continues to evolve, so do the threats that aim to exploit it. As you contemplate your organization's technical safeguards, consider their effectiveness in the face of these evolving threats. Are they up to date? Do they cover all potential vulnerabilities? How often are they reviewed and updated? Reflecting on these questions will guide your efforts towards robust and effective technical safeguards.

Documentation and Record Retention

In the final segment of Chapter 6, we address an often overlooked but vital aspect of securing Electronic Health Information (EHI): Documentation and Record Retention. If the previous safeguards we've discussed are akin to the locks, alarm systems, and secure doors of a building, then think of documentation and record retention as the meticulous records kept by a diligent security guard, noting every entry, exit, and event. These records not only help in tracking and analyzing incidents but also provide evidence of compliance with the HIPAA Security Rule.

The HIPAA Security Rule states that covered entities must "retain the documentation (that is, policies and procedures, actions, activities, and assessments) required by the Security Rule for 6 years from the date of its creation or the date when it last was in effect, whichever is later."

Documentation and record retention encompass several key areas:

Policies and Procedures: All the policies and procedures related to the implementation of the HIPAA Security Rule should be documented. This includes policies about access control, audit controls, integrity controls, authentication, and transmission security.

For example, a hospital might have a detailed policy about access control, specifying who has access to what kind of EHI, how this access is granted, changed, and revoked, and how emergencies are handled.

Actions, Activities, Assessments: Any action, activity, or assessment in compliance with the Security Rule should be documented. This includes risk analysis, risk management activities, sanctions against workforce members for non-compliance, and information system activity reviews.

Take, for instance, a healthcare provider who conducts regular risk analyses to identify potential vulnerabilities in their EHI security. These analyses and the actions taken in response should be thoroughly documented and retained.

Updates and Revisions: Changes and updates to the policies, procedures, and other documentation should also be recorded. The records should reflect the most recent document version and any prior versions.

Let's consider a healthcare insurance company that updates its EHI transmission security policies to incorporate new technology. The company should document these changes and retain the previous versions for reference and compliance verification.

Availability: The documentation should be available to those responsible for implementing the procedures to which the documentation pertains.

For example, a hospital's IT department should have access to documentation related to technical safeguards, allowing them to implement, manage, and update these safeguards effectively.

Review and Update: Documentation should be periodically reviewed and updated in response to environmental or operational changes affecting the security of the EHI.

Consider a clinic that moves to a new location. This change might require updating physical safeguards and the associated documentation to reflect the new environment.

Documentation and record retention play a critical role in maintaining HIPAA compliance and enhancing EHI security. These records provide a roadmap to your organization's compliance journey, signposting what has been done and what needs to be done. As you consider your own documentation and record retention, contemplate their comprehensiveness, accessibility, and responsiveness to change. Regular reviews and updates will ensure your records remain a valuable tool in your HIPAA compliance toolkit.

Breach Notification and Reporting

Identifying and Responding to Breaches

Let's begin Chapter 7 by addressing a scenario that every healthcare organization hopes to avoid: a breach of Protected Health Information (PHI). While our efforts to this point have focused on prevention, it's equally crucial to know how to identify a breach and respond effectively. If the previous chapters have focused on building and maintaining the fortress that protects PHI, then this chapter is about what to do when the fortress walls are breached.

The HIPAA Breach Notification Rule defines a breach as "an impermissible use or disclosure under the Privacy Rule that compromises the security or privacy of the protected health information." In other words, a breach occurs when PHI is accessed, used, disclosed, or disposed of in a way that is not compliant with HIPAA rules, and this violation poses a significant risk of financial, reputational, or other harm to the individual.

Identifying and responding to breaches involves several key steps:

Breach Detection: The first step in managing a breach is identifying it. This could be through an audit, a workforce member reporting a lost or stolen device, a patient complaint, or even a report from a business associate. Regular audits and employee training can help organizations detect breaches promptly.

For example, in 2018, a major U.S. hospital identified a breach when an unauthorized individual gained access to two employees' email accounts, potentially compromising PHI of nearly 14,000 patients. The breach was identified through the hospital's routine audit processes.

Risk Assessment: Once a breach is detected, it's crucial to conduct a risk assessment to determine the nature and extent of the breach, the type of PHI involved, who the unauthorized recipients or users were, and whether the PHI was actually acquired or viewed.

In 2015, health insurer Anthem Inc. discovered that hackers had breached their database and potentially accessed personal information of about 78.8 million people. Anthem's risk assessment revealed that names, dates of birth, social security numbers, healthcare IDs, home addresses, email addresses, and employment information were potentially accessed.

Containment and Remediation: After assessing the risk, the organization should take steps to limit the damage. This could involve shutting down a compromised server, changing access credentials, retrieving lost devices, or even notifying law enforcement in cases of cyberattacks.

In the Anthem breach, the company worked closely with the FBI, increased its security measures, and provided free credit monitoring and identity theft repair services to the affected individuals.

Notification: If a breach affects more than 500 individuals, the HIPAA Breach Notification Rule requires the covered entity to notify the affected individuals, the Secretary of Health and Human Services (HHS), and the media without unreasonable delay and in no case later than 60 days following the discovery of a breach.

Following the breach, Anthem promptly notified the affected individuals and the HHS and issued a press release about the breach.

Remember, breaches can be costly, both in terms of potential civil penalties and the loss of patient trust. Therefore, effective identification and response to breaches are critical for any HIPAA compliance program. As we delve deeper into this chapter, consider how well-equipped your organization is to detect and manage breaches. Is there room for improvement? How can you build upon your existing strategies?

Notification Requirements and Timelines

This section stands as your map and compass, delineating the obligations and timelines set forth by the HIPAA Breach Notification Rule. As we journey through these details, keep in mind that timely, appropriate notification is not just a legal requirement – it's also a vital part of maintaining trust with patients and the broader community.

The notification requirements depend on the number of individuals affected by the breach.

For breaches affecting fewer than 500 individuals, the covered entity must notify the affected individuals without unreasonable delay and in no case later than 60 days following the discovery of a breach. However, it's encouraged to notify affected individuals as soon as possible. The covered entity must also keep a log or other documentation of such breaches and, not later than 60 days after the end of each calendar year, provide the Secretary of HHS with such a log.

For breaches affecting 500 or more individuals, the covered entity must notify the affected individuals, the Secretary of HHS, and, in some cases, the media, without unreasonable delay and in no case later than 60 days following the discovery of a breach. Notification to the Secretary should be done concurrently with notification to the individuals. In cases where the affected individuals exceed 500 residents of a state or jurisdiction, prominent media outlets serving the state or jurisdiction must also be notified.

The notification must include, to the extent possible:

1. **A brief description of the breach**, including the dates of the breach and its discovery, if known.
2. **A description of the types of unsecured PHI** involved in the breach.
3. **Steps individuals should take to protect themselves** from potential harm resulting from the breach.
4. **A description of what the covered entity is doing** to investigate the breach, mitigate harm, and prevent further breaches.
5. **Contact information for individuals** to ask questions or learn additional information, which must include a toll-free telephone number, an email address, website, or postal address.

The timeline for notification begins when the breach is first discovered, not when the investigation is complete. A breach is considered discovered on the first day it is known, or by exercising reasonable diligence would have been known, to any person (other than the person committing the breach) who is a workforce member or agent of the covered entity or business associate.

HIPAA's stringent timelines underscore the gravity of a breach and the urgency with which it must be addressed. As we continue this journey into breach notification and reporting, consider how these requirements align with your current practices. Are your systems equipped to meet these requirements? How might you improve your breach response and notification process?

Reporting Breaches to the Office for Civil Rights (OCR)

Imagine standing on a precipice, peering over the edge at the aftermath of a breach. Notifying the affected individuals is only one part of the process. Another critical step that cannot be ignored is reporting the breach to the Office for Civil Rights (OCR). In this section, we'll navigate the labyrinth of requirements for reporting breaches to the OCR, a task that, while perhaps daunting, is an essential part of HIPAA compliance.

The OCR enforces the HIPAA Privacy, Security, and Breach Notification Rules, and reporting breaches to the OCR is a key part of your organization's accountability. The goal here is not to add more stress to an already challenging situation but to ensure transparency, responsibility, and ultimately, the protection of patient rights.

The reporting process varies depending on the scale of the breach:

Breaches Affecting Fewer Than 500 Individuals: For smaller breaches, covered entities must maintain a log or other documentation of the breaches and, within 60 days after the end of the calendar year, report them to the OCR. Reports are submitted through the OCR's web portal, and each breach must be reported separately.

Breaches Affecting 500 or More Individuals: Larger breaches must be reported to the OCR without unreasonable delay and in no case later than 60 days from the discovery of the breach. Like smaller breaches, these are also reported through the OCR's web portal. However, the urgency is greater, and the report must coincide with notifications to the affected individuals.

When reporting breaches to the OCR, your organization must provide:

- **Contact Information**: For the covered entity (or business associate) and the person reporting the breach.
- **Breach Description**: Details about the breach, including the date of the breach and discovery, the type of breach (e.g., theft, unauthorized access), location of the breach, and the type of PHI involved.
- **Individuals Affected**: The number of individuals affected by the breach.
- **Corrective Action Taken**: Steps the covered entity took upon discovery of the breach, including efforts to mitigate harm.

Let's consider the breach of Premera Blue Cross in 2015, one of the largest healthcare data breaches in U.S. history.

In spring of 2014, a phishing email enabled hackers to install malware on Premera's systems that gave them access to its members' data. The breach went undetected for nearly nine months, until January 2015. In March, PBC reported the breach to OCR.

The undetected advanced persistent threat attack led to the disclosure of more than 10.4 million individuals' protected health information including their names, addresses, dates of birth, email addresses, Social Security numbers, bank account information and health plan clinical information.

Announced just a month after another breach had hit another insurer, Anthem, the Premera incident was one of the earlier major salvos in what would soon become a sustained attack on U.S. healthcare organizations – serving as confirmation that hospitals and health plans were in the crosshairs of cybercriminals worldwide. Premera's swift action and transparent communication set an example for how to handle such a critical situation.

Bear in mind that thorough, accurate reporting to the OCR is not just about fulfilling a regulatory obligation. It's about being accountable to your patients, your employees, and the community you serve. As we further explore the intricacies of breach notification and reporting, reflect on how your organization is prepared to handle this responsibility. How can you ensure timely, accurate, and thorough reporting if a breach occurs?

Working with Business Associates

Business Associate Agreements (BAAs)

Just as a skilled conductor leads an orchestra, ensuring harmony among the players, so too must healthcare entities manage their relationships with business associates. This section takes us on a journey through the intricacies of Business Associate Agreements (BAAs), a critical piece of the HIPAA compliance puzzle. Like a maestro's baton, BAAs guide the performance, specifying the roles and responsibilities of each party, and ensuring the symphony of data protection plays on, uninterrupted.

Under HIPAA, covered entities are required to sign a Business Associate Agreement (BAA) with any business associate (BA) that will create, receive, maintain, or transmit Protected Health Information (PHI) on their behalf. BAs can include a wide range of entities or individuals, from billing companies and consultants to IT providers and shredding companies.

The BAA is more than just a contract; it is a testament to your commitment to protecting your patients' privacy and health information.

Key elements of a BAA include:

- **Description of Permitted and Required Uses of PHI**: The BAA must clearly outline what the BA is permitted to do with the PHI, what it is required to do, and that it will not use or further disclose the PHI other than as permitted or required by the agreement or as required by law.
- **Safeguards**: The BAA must specify that the BA will use appropriate safeguards to prevent unauthorized use or disclosure of the PHI.
- **Reporting**: The BAA must stipulate that the BA will report to the covered entity any use or disclosure of the PHI not provided for by its contract, including breaches of unsecured PHI, and any security incident of which it becomes aware.
- **Subcontractors**: The BAA must ensure that the BA will ensure that any subcontractors it may engage on its behalf that will have access to PHI agree to the same restrictions and conditions.
- **Access and Amendment**: Where necessary for the covered entity to fulfill its obligations under the Privacy Rule, the BAA must provide for the BA to make PHI available for access and amendment by the individual.
- **Accounting of Disclosures**: The BAA must provide that the BA will document disclosures of PHI and information related to such disclosures as would be required for the covered entity to respond to a request by an individual for an accounting of disclosures of PHI.
- **Termination**: The BAA must authorize termination of the contract by the covered entity if the covered entity determines that the BA has violated a material term of the agreement.

An excellent example of a BAA in action is the case of North Memorial Health Care of Minnesota, which failed to establish a

BAA with a major contractor, resulting in a breach of unsecured PHI of 9,497 patients. The OCR levied a hefty $1.55 million settlement. This case underscores the importance of having a robust, comprehensive BAA in place.

As we navigate the world of BAAs and their critical role in HIPAA compliance, consider your current BA relationships. Do you have BAAs in place with all necessary parties? How might your existing agreements be strengthened to better protect your organization and the data you are entrusted with?

Let's see how an example of a BAA might look like:

BUSINESS ASSOCIATE AGREEMENT (BAA)

THIS AGREEMENT is made this day of _____, 2023, between _____ (hereinafter referred to as "Covered Entity") and _____ (hereinafter referred to as "Business Associate").

1. *Description of Permitted and Required Uses of PHI*
   1.1 The Business Associate shall not use or further disclose PHI other than as permitted or required by this Agreement or as required by law. The Business Associate may use or disclose PHI to perform functions, activities, or services specified in the underlying service agreement, provided such use or disclosure does not violate the HIPAA Privacy Rule.

2. *Safeguards*
   2.1 The Business Associate shall implement and use appropriate safeguards to prevent unauthorized use or disclosure of PHI, including implementing requirements of the HIPAA Security Rule pertaining to administrative, physical, and technical safeguards.

3. *Reporting*

   3.1 The Business Associate shall report to the Covered Entity any use or disclosure of PHI not provided for by this Agreement, including breaches of unsecured PHI as required at 45 CFR 164.410, and any security incident of which it becomes aware, in accordance with 45 CFR 164.314(a)(2)(i)(C).

4. *Subcontractors*

   4.1 In accordance with 45 CFR 164.502(e)(1)(ii) and 164.308(b)(2), the Business Associate shall ensure that any subcontractors that create, receive, maintain, or transmit PHI on behalf of the Business Associate agree to the same restrictions, conditions, and requirements that apply to the Business Associate.

5. *Access and Amendment*

   5.1 The Business Associate shall provide access, at the request of the Covered Entity, and in the time and manner designated by the Covered Entity, to PHI in a Designated Record Set, to the Covered Entity or, as directed by the Covered Entity, to an Individual in order to meet the requirements under 45 CFR 164.524.

   5.2 The Business Associate shall make any amendments to PHI in a Designated Record Set that the Covered Entity directs or agrees to pursuant to 45 CFR 164.526 at the request of the Covered Entity or an Individual.

6. *Accounting of Disclosures*

   6.1 The Business Associate shall document disclosures of PHI and information related to such disclosures as would be required for the Covered Entity to respond to a request by an Individual for an accounting of disclosures of PHI in accordance with 45 CFR 164.528.

7. *Termination*

7.1 Upon the Covered Entity's knowledge of a material breach by the Business Associate, the Covered Entity shall either:

(a) Provide an opportunity for the Business Associate to cure the breach or end the violation, and terminate the contract if the Business Associate does not cure the breach or end the violation within the specified time; or

(b) Immediately terminate the contract if the Business Associate has breached a material term of the contract and cure is not possible.

IN WITNESS WHEREOF, the parties hereto have duly executed this Agreement as of the date first above written.

Covered Entity_____

Business Associate_____

Disclaimer: This is a simplified example of a Business Associate Agreement and does not cover all the necessary provisions or legal requirements of a HIPAA-compliant contract. You should consult with a qualified legal professional or a HIPAA consultant to ensure your Business Associate Agreement is comprehensive and compliant with all applicable laws and regulations.

Ensuring Business Associates are HIPAA Compliant

In the world of healthcare, relationships are everything. The bond between a doctor and patient, the rapport among colleagues, and the tie between healthcare providers and their business associates (BAs) – each one is vital. But one of these relationships carries with it a unique set of responsibilities and risks: the relationship with

BAs. In this section, we turn our attention to the task of ensuring that BAs are HIPAA compliant, a crucial component of any robust compliance program.

Working with BAs who handle Protected Health Information (PHI) is like passing the baton in a relay race. You need to have confidence that they will carry it forward without dropping it. Translated to HIPAA context, this means ensuring that your BAs are HIPAA compliant.

While you cannot directly control how BAs manage the data they handle on your behalf, you can take steps to ensure they understand and commit to HIPAA compliance:

Conduct Due Diligence: Before engaging with a BA, conduct due diligence to understand their data protection practices. Ask for references, explore their history of data breaches, and request documentation of their privacy and security practices.

Provide Training: Although BAs are expected to provide HIPAA training to their employees, you can offer supplemental training or resources to ensure they understand your specific expectations and procedures.

Monitor Compliance: Regular audits of your BAs can help identify potential compliance issues before they become problems. These audits might include reviewing policies, procedures, and training records, as well as conducting onsite visits.

Establish Clear Communication Channels: Ensure that your BAs know who to contact in your organization if they have questions or concerns about HIPAA compliance or if a breach occurs. Prompt communication can often mitigate potential harm.

Incorporate Penalties in BAAs: Your BAAs should clearly outline the penalties for non-compliance with HIPAA rules, potentially including financial penalties or termination of the contract.

Let's consider the case of Oregon Health & Science University (OHSU), which reported two breaches involving BAs. The OCR investigation revealed significant risk-management failures, including the lack of a BAA with a cloud storage service provider. OHSU agreed to pay $2.7 million and implement a corrective action plan. This case highlights the importance of ensuring your BAs are HIPAA compliant.

Monitoring and Auditing Business Associate Relationships

Imagine you're at the helm of a ship on a moonless night, navigating through treacherous waters. It's not enough to set a course and hope for the best. You must constantly monitor your position, adjust your course, and be ready to respond to any unexpected challenges. This is much like monitoring and auditing your relationships with Business Associates (BAs). In this section, we focus on these proactive practices, the lighthouse guiding your organization safely through the potential hazards of non-compliance.

Ensuring that your BAs remain compliant with HIPAA regulations requires ongoing oversight. Signing the Business Associate Agreement (BAA) is not the end of the journey, but rather the beginning. Active monitoring and auditing play an essential role in this ongoing process. Here's how you can effectively monitor and audit your BA relationships:

Develop a Monitoring Plan: This plan should define what you will monitor, how frequently, and who will do the monitoring. The monitoring activities might include regular reviews of BA reports, random audits, or automated system checks.

Conduct Regular Audits: Audits should be performed regularly, and the frequency might depend on the level of risk associated with the particular BA. For example, a BA that handles a large volume of PHI might warrant more frequent audits than one that handles minimal data.

Follow a Standard Audit Procedure: This could include reviewing the BA's policies and procedures, checking that employees have been trained, and confirming that the BA is appropriately safeguarding PHI. Using a standard procedure ensures consistency and makes it easier to compare results over time or across BAs.

Document Your Findings: Keep detailed records of your monitoring and auditing activities. This will provide a historical record that can be useful for future audits and can provide evidence of your due diligence in the event of a breach or an audit by the Office for Civil Rights (OCR).

Act on Your Findings: If your monitoring or auditing activities reveal potential problems, take action to address them. This might include providing additional training, revising procedures, or in extreme cases, terminating the relationship with the BA.

Let's take a look at the case of Raleigh Orthopedic Clinic, P.A., of North Carolina. They handed over X-ray films of 17,300 patients to a BA who promised to transfer the images to electronic media in return for harvesting the silver from the X-ray films. However, the clinic failed to execute a BAA with the BA, resulting in a potential breach. An OCR investigation resulted in a settlement of $750,000 with the clinic, reinforcing the importance of monitoring and auditing BA relationships.

As you consider the strategies for monitoring and auditing BA relationships, reflect on your organization's current practices. How often do you audit your BAs? What does your monitoring process look like? Are there areas where you could improve?

HIPAA Enforcement and Penalties

OCR Investigations and Audits

A specter is haunting the world of healthcare - the specter of HIPAA non-compliance. It can strike fear into the hearts of even the most seasoned healthcare professionals. Yet, fear is often born of the unknown, and in this section, I aim to make the unknown known. Here, we'll demystify the process of OCR investigations and audits, bringing clarity to what can often feel like a daunting and uncertain process.

The Office for Civil Rights (OCR) is the arm of the Department of Health and Human Services (HHS) that oversees enforcement of HIPAA regulations. The OCR carries out its mandate through two primary mechanisms: investigations and audits.

OCR Investigations

OCR investigations are typically initiated in response to a complaint or a reported breach affecting 500 or more individuals. Here's what you need to know about the process:

Initiation: A complaint or breach report triggers an investigation. Anyone can file a complaint, and covered entities are required to report breaches affecting 500 or more individuals.

Inquiry: The OCR will send an inquiry to the covered entity asking for more information about the alleged violation. The entity's response will largely determine the course of the investigation.

Investigation: If the initial response is inadequate, a full investigation may ensue. This could involve reviewing documents, interviewing staff, and assessing the entity's HIPAA compliance efforts.

Resolution: If the OCR determines that a violation occurred, it will seek to resolve the case. This could involve a corrective action plan, a resolution agreement, or civil money penalties.

OCR Audits

OCR audits, on the other hand, are proactive measures designed to evaluate compliance efforts across the healthcare industry. They are not typically triggered by specific complaints or breaches. Here's what you need to know:

Selection: The OCR selects entities for audit based on a variety of factors, including the entity's size, type, and past compliance history.

Notification: The selected entity will receive a notification of its upcoming audit. The notification will include information about the scope of the audit and the documents the entity will need to provide.

Audit: The OCR will conduct the audit, which might involve a site visit, interviews, and document review.

Report: After the audit, the OCR will provide the entity with a draft report. The entity will have an opportunity to respond to the report before it is finalized.

Resolution: If the audit reveals significant compliance issues, the OCR may initiate an investigation, which could lead to a corrective action plan or penalties.

To give you a real-world scenario, consider the case of Memorial Healthcare System (MHS). In 2012, MHS reported that its employees had impermissibly accessed patient information. The subsequent OCR investigation discovered that MHS had failed to implement procedures to regularly review records of information system activity. MHS agreed to a $5.5 million settlement and a robust corrective action plan.

As we traverse the terrain of OCR investigations and audits, consider your organization's readiness. How would you respond to an OCR inquiry today? Are your policies and procedures robust enough to withstand an audit?

I always encourage people to be proactive instead of reactive, and I hope that at this point you can already see the benefits of adopting a proactive approach for being HIPAA compliant (the same applies for any other law, regulation, standard or framework that your entity needs to report compliance with), if you need to "react" most likely is already too late. -Just personal opinion here.

Types of Penalties and Fines

To fully appreciate the weight of HIPAA compliance, one must understand the potential consequences of non-compliance. At the intersection of law and healthcare, the journey doesn't end with just understanding the regulations - it's equally crucial to comprehend the repercussions if those regulations are not met.

HIPAA violations come with significant penalties, both monetary and non-monetary. The cost of non-compliance can be steep, impacting not just an organization's bottom line, but also its reputation and trustworthiness.

Monetary Penalties

The Department of Health and Human Services (HHS) has established a tiered civil penalty system - the seriousness of the violation and the violator's knowledge of the violation determine the amount of the fine:

Tier 1: Unknowing violations. The covered entity or individual did not know and, by exercising reasonable diligence, would not have known of the violation. Fines range from $100 to $50,000 per violation, with a maximum of $1.5 million per year for violations of an identical provision.

Tier 2: Reasonable cause violations. The violation was due to reasonable cause and not willful neglect. Fines range from $1,000 to $50,000 per violation, with a maximum of $1.5 million per year for violations of an identical provision.

Tier 3: Willful neglect violations that are corrected. The violation was due to willful neglect, but the violation was corrected within a specified time period. Fines range from $10,000 to $50,000 per violation, with a maximum of $1.5 million per year for violations of an identical provision.

Tier 4: Willful neglect violations that are not corrected. The violation was due to willful neglect, and the violation was not corrected. Fines are $50,000 per violation, with a maximum of $1.5 million per year for violations of an identical provision.

Non-Monetary Penalties

In addition to the financial penalties, there are non-monetary consequences for HIPAA violations:

Corrective Action Plans (CAPs): If a violation is found, the OCR can require a covered entity or business associate to implement a

CAP to address the deficiencies in its HIPAA compliance program and prevent future violations.

Loss of Business: Violations can lead to a loss of trust from patients and partners, resulting in a loss of business.

Criminal Penalties: In some cases, individuals can face criminal charges for HIPAA violations, including jail time.

Take as an example, the case of Cignet Health of Prince George's County, MD. They were fined $4.3 million for denying 41 patients access to their medical records and then failing to cooperate with the OCR's investigations. The penalty was a combination of the baseline fine for the violation itself and an additional fine for the lack of cooperation during the investigation.

In this journey through the possible penalties and fines associated with HIPAA non-compliance, remember that the goal is not just to avoid fines, but to protect patient information, uphold the law, and maintain the trust of those you serve.

Corrective Action Plans

It's said that in life, it's not about the mistakes we make, but rather how we rectify them. In the realm of HIPAA compliance, this philosophy takes form through the implementation of Corrective Action Plans (CAPs). CAPs are not merely a reactive measure to HIPAA violations but are a beacon of learning and a roadmap to better patient data protection.

A Corrective Action Plan is the result of an investigation by the Office for Civil Rights (OCR) after a breach or complaint has been filed. If non-compliance is determined, the OCR will require the covered entity or business associate to develop a CAP as part of the settlement agreement.

Components of a Corrective Action Plan

A CAP typically includes the following elements:

1. **Detailed Description of the Issue**: The CAP should provide an in-depth understanding of the non-compliance issue. This includes the nature of the violation, how it was discovered, and the impact it had on the affected parties.
2. **Remediation Measures**: The entity must outline the specific steps they will take to rectify the issue. This could involve changes in processes, systems, or even personnel training to ensure the same violation doesn't occur again.
3. **Timeframe for Implementation**: Each corrective measure will have a specified deadline for completion. The entity will have to report back to the OCR demonstrating that the remediation has been successfully implemented within this timeframe.
4. **Proof of Compliance**: This often involves providing documentation, records, or other forms of evidence to show that the entity is now operating in accordance with HIPAA requirements.

Consider the case of Anchorage Community Mental Health Services (ACMHS). After suffering a breach that affected 2,743 individuals due to malware, ACMHS agreed to a settlement with OCR that included a $150,000 fine and a CAP. The CAP included, among other things, updating policies and procedures, staff training, and regular reporting to OCR.

The process of creating and implementing a CAP can be challenging, but it's also an opportunity. It's an opportunity to learn from past mistakes, to reassess and reevaluate existing practices, and to strengthen the commitment to HIPAA compliance. It emphasizes the principle that HIPAA compliance isn't a one-time task but a continuous journey that evolves with time, technology, and our growing understanding of privacy and security.

Best Practices for Avoiding Violations

Just as a well-versed sailor navigates the open seas with a keen understanding of potential storms and how to steer clear of them, so too must healthcare organizations voyage through the landscape of HIPAA compliance. The best defense against violations is a proactive approach to compliance, armed with strategies that are designed to pre-empt potential pitfalls.

Maintain Up-to-Date Policies and Procedures

One of the most effective deterrents against violations is a robust set of policies and procedures that reflect the latest HIPAA regulations. These documents should be living, breathing entities within your organization - reviewed regularly, updated when necessary, and disseminated effectively to all relevant personnel.

Invest in Regular Training

Even the best policies are worthless if your staff members don't understand them. Regular, comprehensive training on HIPAA regulations, organization-specific policies, and real-world scenarios is a must. Remember, ignorance of the law is not an excuse for non-compliance.

Perform Regular Risk Assessments

A HIPAA risk assessment is more than a checkbox on your compliance to-do list - it's a powerful tool for identifying vulnerabilities in your organization's PHI safeguards. By identifying these risks before they result in breaches, you can take steps to mitigate them proactively.

Encrypt, Encrypt, Encrypt

Encryption is a critical component of HIPAA compliance, particularly in the context of electronic PHI. By encrypting data both in transit and at rest, you can significantly reduce the risk of a breach.

Plan for the Worst

Even with the best defenses, violations can still occur. Having a response plan in place can help mitigate the damage. This includes processes for identifying and containing the breach, notifying affected individuals and the OCR, and implementing a corrective action plan.

Promote a Culture of Compliance

Ultimately, HIPAA compliance isn't about ticking boxes - it's about fostering a culture that respects the privacy and security of patient information. When compliance becomes a core value rather than an imposed requirement, avoiding violations becomes a natural byproduct of your organization's operations.

Consider the story of a small clinic in Oregon. Through proactive HIPAA training, they discovered that their system for disposing of patient records was not HIPAA-compliant. They were able to correct the issue before it resulted in a breach, demonstrating the power of proactive compliance.

As we continue our journey through the realm of HIPAA compliance, remember that every aspect of your organization - from your IT infrastructure to your front-desk staff - plays a vital role in safeguarding PHI. There's no one-size-fits-all approach to avoiding violations; it's a combination of the right strategies tailored to the unique characteristics of your organization.

HIPAA in the Digital Age

Telehealth and Remote Patient Monitoring

The dawn of the 21st century, accompanied by a whirlwind of digital innovations, has redrawn the healthcare landscape. We've embarked on an exciting journey into an era of healthcare where physicians can monitor their patients' health from afar, and consultations can happen across continents. Yes, we are talking about Telehealth and Remote Patient Monitoring, two critical components of modern healthcare. But as we traverse this brave new world of digital healthcare, we must remember our steadfast companion - HIPAA.

Telehealth: Delivering Care Across the Digital Divide

Telehealth, a term that encompasses a wide range of remote healthcare services, is no longer a futuristic concept. It's here, it's real, and it's transforming lives. From video consultations to remote chronic disease management, telehealth is breaking down geographical barriers and making healthcare more accessible.

But with this convenience and accessibility comes the responsibility of maintaining patient privacy and data security. HIPAA compliance remains paramount. Video consultations, for instance, require HIPAA-compliant software that encrypts data during transmission. It's not just about the software, though. The physical location of the healthcare provider during the consultation, the security of the networks they use - everything factors into HIPAA compliance.

Remote Patient Monitoring: Keeping an Eye on Health

Remote patient monitoring (RPM) takes telehealth a step further, allowing healthcare providers to monitor patients' health data in real-time. Imagine a cardiologist instantly receiving an alert when a patient's heart rate spikes, or a diabetic's glucose levels being continuously tracked and managed. The possibilities are profound.

Yet, as inspiring as these possibilities are, the privacy and security implications are equally significant. With RPM, a wealth of sensitive patient data is being transmitted, often continuously, between devices and healthcare providers. Protecting this data, both in transit and at rest, is crucial. HIPAA-compliant technologies and practices must be used to ensure the integrity and confidentiality of this information.

To illustrate, let's look at a remote cardiac monitoring company that implemented a HIPAA-compliant RPM solution. They used encrypted devices to transmit data, secured their networks, and trained staff on HIPAA requirements. As a result, they were able to provide their services without compromising patient privacy.

As we forge ahead into a future where digital and health intersect more frequently and profoundly, HIPAA's role in safeguarding patient information becomes even more critical. Whether it's a video consultation or remote disease management, HIPAA compliance isn't just a legal obligation - it's an essential component of patient trust in the digital age.

Mobile Apps and Wearables

In the contemporary age, our lives have been enriched, and our routines streamlined, by the boom of mobile applications and wearable technologies. They have not only redefined convenience but also created new dimensions for healthcare. From apps that track calories and steps to wearables monitoring heart rates and sleep patterns, our health insights are more accessible than ever. But with great data comes great responsibility, and that's where HIPAA steps in to ensure this digital revolution respects privacy and confidentiality.

Mobile Health Apps: Your Health at Your Fingertips

Mobile health apps have brought the power of health management to our pockets. Need to track your blood pressure, manage medication schedules, or consult a diet chart? There's an app for that. But each of these apps potentially handles sensitive health information, and thus, must adhere to HIPAA regulations.

Consider a popular diabetes management app that stores and analyses glucose readings, food intake, and insulin doses. It's essential that the app developer ensures data security at all stages, including data entry, storage, and transmission. The data must be encrypted, and any third-party services used, such as cloud storage providers, must also be HIPAA compliant.

Wearables: A Step Ahead in Personal Health Monitoring

Wearable technology has taken personal health monitoring to a new level. Today's fitness trackers, smartwatches, and even smart clothing can track an array of health parameters, from the number of steps you take to your heart rate variability.

However, these wearables pose unique challenges in terms of HIPAA compliance. Not all wearables are covered by HIPAA, as it depends on who collects the data and for what purpose. If the data is shared with a covered entity such as a healthcare provider, then it falls under HIPAA's purview. For instance, if a smartwatch company shares heart rate data with a user's cardiologist, that data must be handled according to HIPAA regulations.

Let's take the example of a company that designed a wearable device for cardiac patients. The device continuously monitors heart rate and rhythm, and the data is shared with healthcare providers for analysis. To ensure HIPAA compliance, the company used end-to-end encryption for data transmission, stored data securely with a HIPAA-compliant cloud service and implemented strict access controls.

The law continues to serve as a sturdy guardrail, ensuring our health data remains confidential and secure as we embrace the convenience of mobile apps and wearables.

Health Data Privacy in Social Media and Online Forums

Unfurling the vast, intricate web of digital communication, we find ourselves at the juncture of social media and online forums. These platforms offer the global community an unparalleled opportunity to share, learn, and engage. However, this digital openness also presents unique challenges to health data privacy, making it a critical piece of the HIPAA compliance puzzle.

Navigating the Social Media Maze

Social media platforms can serve as a powerful tool for healthcare providers to share valuable health information, facilitate patient engagement, and even provide telehealth services. However, with the potential of reaching millions comes the responsibility of protecting the privacy of those engaged.

Imagine a healthcare provider tweeting about a rare disease case they handled. Even if they don't name the patient, if the details provided are specific enough to identify the patient, it would constitute a HIPAA violation. Therefore, all health-related communication on social media must be carefully crafted to avoid sharing any identifiable health information unless explicit patient consent has been obtained.

It's also crucial for healthcare providers to implement robust social media policies and training programs to ensure all employees understand what constitutes a HIPAA violation in the context of social media. For example, even a well-intentioned Facebook post by a hospital employee about a patient's recovery could violate HIPAA if done without consent.

Online Forums: A Double-Edged Sword

Online forums have emerged as a popular platform for individuals to share health experiences and seek advice. They can be an invaluable resource for patients dealing with chronic diseases or rare conditions. However, these platforms also pose significant challenges for health data privacy.

Anonymity is a key factor in the realm of online forums. While users may post about their health issues under pseudonyms, the risk of re-identification should not be overlooked. For instance, if a user shares detailed health information on a public forum, a data scientist might cross-reference this data with other publicly available data to identify the user.

Furthermore, forum moderators should be mindful of their responsibilities. If a forum is sponsored by a covered entity and involves the sharing of PHI, it may be subject to HIPAA regulations. For example, if a hospital hosts a forum for patients to discuss their experiences with a particular treatment, the hospital must ensure the discussion complies with HIPAA.

Managing Consent and Expectations

In a world where sharing is often synonymous with caring, it's essential to set clear boundaries and manage expectations in the digital realm. Patients need to understand that while sharing personal health information online can have benefits, it can also expose them to privacy risks. Healthcare providers, in turn, should help patients make informed decisions about what they choose to share online.

This is where a well-articulated and easily accessible social media policy comes in. Such a policy should clearly outline what kind of information can be shared, how it will be used, and what controls the patient has over their information. It should also clarify what the potential risks of sharing personal health information online are, including the risk of re-identification.

Adapting to Rapid Technological Change

As technology continues to evolve, so do the challenges related to health data privacy. The adoption of new technologies, such as AI, machine learning, and blockchain, can both help and hinder efforts to maintain privacy.

Artificial Intelligence (AI) and machine learning can help detect potential HIPAA violations or suspicious activities that could lead to data breaches. For instance, AI could identify patterns of behavior that indicate an employee is accessing patient records without authorization.

On the other hand, technologies like blockchain, while promising enhanced security for health data, also raise new privacy concerns. If a blockchain system is used to store health data, it's crucial to ensure that the information is thoroughly de-identified and cannot be linked back to the patient.

In conclusion, when it comes to health data privacy on social media and online forums, a balanced approach is necessary. It is about fostering open, beneficial discussions while also taking diligent steps to protect individuals' privacy. This delicate balance, when achieved, not only upholds the principles of HIPAA but also enriches the very fabric of our digital society.

Emerging Technologies and Future Challenges

Embarking on the final leg of our exploration in Chapter 10, we find ourselves face-to-face with the future. In "Emerging Technologies and Future Challenges," we take a visionary leap forward, exploring the innovative technologies on the horizon and the challenges they present to the time-tested principles of HIPAA.

Artificial Intelligence and Machine Learning

Artificial Intelligence (AI) and Machine Learning (ML) are more than just buzzwords. They're transformative technologies that are reshaping every aspect of our lives, including healthcare. From predictive analytics in patient care to automated administrative tasks, AI and ML have a broad range of applications in healthcare.

While these technologies offer immense potential, they also bring unique challenges to HIPAA compliance. For instance, AI systems often require large volumes of data to function effectively, potentially increasing the risk of data breaches. Additionally, AI algorithms can sometimes 'learn' to identify individuals from data that was thought to be de-identified, a phenomenon known as re-identification.

Healthcare organizations must, therefore, be proactive in conducting risk assessments when implementing these technologies, ensuring that all AI and ML use cases are in compliance with HIPAA regulations.

Blockchain Technology

Blockchain technology, best known for its use in cryptocurrencies, offers promising applications in healthcare, specifically in ensuring data integrity and traceability. Its decentralized, immutable nature makes it an appealing solution for health information exchange, patient consent management, and even combating counterfeit drugs.

However, the very feature that makes blockchain secure—the unalterable recording of data—also raises significant HIPAA concerns. If protected health information (PHI) were to be recorded on a blockchain, it would be nearly impossible to delete, potentially conflicting with HIPAA's regulations on the right to amend and the right to be forgotten.

Furthermore, while data on a blockchain can be encrypted, it can still be a tempting target for cybercriminals. Healthcare entities looking to implement blockchain must ensure that additional safeguards are in place to protect PHI.

Internet of Things (IoT)

The Internet of Things (IoT), which refers to the network of physical devices connected to the internet, has seen substantial growth in healthcare. From wearable fitness trackers to smart insulin pumps, IoT devices have the potential to improve patient outcomes and personalize care.

But with great connectivity comes great responsibility. IoT devices are notorious for their security vulnerabilities, and healthcare IoT is no exception. These devices can be easy targets for hackers and can serve as entry points into a healthcare organization's network. Ensuring these devices are secure and that the data they collect and transmit is protected according to HIPAA regulations is a significant challenge.

11

Maintaining Compliance and Adapting to Changes

Ongoing risk assessments

With Chapter 11, we are entering the culminating stage of our journey through the complex yet imperative world of HIPAA compliance. This chapter, "Maintaining Compliance and Adapting to Changes," will equip us with tools and insights to keep our organizations aligned with the evolving landscape of health information privacy. In this first section, we turn our focus to the cornerstone of this adaptive process - "Ongoing Risk Assessments".

The Imperative of Continual Risk Assessment

Ongoing risk assessment is not just a recommendation, but a requirement under the Security Rule of HIPAA. It's not enough to perform a one-time assessment; healthcare organizations must continuously monitor and evaluate their security controls and practices to identify and mitigate new and evolving risks to electronic Protected Health Information (ePHI).

Risk assessments should be performed regularly and should also follow any significant changes in the organization's environment, such as a major IT overhaul, an acquisition, or the introduction of new health services. Failure to carry out these assessments can leave an organization vulnerable to breaches and subsequent penalties.

Components of an Effective Risk Assessment

A comprehensive risk assessment encompasses four key elements:

1. **Identifying the ePHI**: The first step is to understand where all ePHI is stored, received, maintained, or transmitted. This includes not just electronic health records but also billing information, appointment scheduling software, and any other digital tool that handles ePHI.
2. **Identifying Threats and Vulnerabilities**: Once all instances of ePHI have been located, the next step is to identify potential threats to that data—everything from hackers to natural disasters—and vulnerabilities that could be exploited.
3. **Assessing Current Security Measures**: Evaluate the effectiveness of current security measures. These could be encryption, access controls, data backups, and more.
4. **Determining the Likelihood and Impact of Threat Occurrence**: Finally, the risk assessment should determine the probability of potential risks occurring and the impact they would have on the organization.

Documenting the Risk Assessment

Documentation of these risk assessments is crucial. It's not enough to simply perform the risk assessment; the process and results must be meticulously recorded. This documentation serves as proof of compliance in case of an audit and can also guide future risk management activities.

Reviewing and updating policies and procedures

Peeling back the layers of Chapter 11, we now encounter an equally significant aspect of maintaining HIPAA compliance, "Reviewing and Updating Policies and Procedures." In this perpetually evolving digital landscape, static compliance strategies are as ineffective as trying to navigate modern city streets with an outdated map. This section underscores the vitality of keeping our strategies agile, our policies updated, and our procedures under constant scrutiny.

Relevance of Policy and Procedure Updates

In the world of health information privacy and security, complacency can lead to catastrophic results. The continuous evolution of technologies and threat vectors necessitates that policies and procedures be regularly reviewed and updated. The goal is to ensure they reflect the current state of operations and adequately address the risks that the organization faces.

Reviewing Policies and Procedures

Reviewing policies and procedures is not merely a box-ticking exercise. It involves a thorough examination of each policy and procedure to ensure that it aligns with the existing regulatory environment and the organization's operations. It should also assess whether the policy or procedure has been effective in achieving its intended outcome.

For instance, if an organization has a policy regarding access controls but experiences repeated instances of unauthorized access, it's an indication that the policy needs revising. Similarly, if a data backup procedure is in place but recovery is slow or incomplete during a disaster simulation, this signals the need for an update.

Updating Policies and Procedures

Once the review has identified areas of improvement, the next step is to make the necessary updates. This may involve tightening access controls, enhancing data encryption, changing data backup procedures, or implementing stronger user authentication mechanisms.

Moreover, updates should also reflect any changes in the broader context in which the organization operates. These can include shifts in the regulatory landscape, technological advancements, or changes in the threat environment.

Documenting and Communicating Changes

Every change made to policies and procedures should be well-documented. Not only does this serve as evidence of compliance, but it also creates a record that can be referred to in future reviews. It is equally important to communicate these changes to all relevant personnel. After all, a policy or procedure can only be effective if those who are expected to follow it are fully aware of what it entails.

Staying informed about regulatory updates

Plunging further into the depths of Chapter 11, we reach the critical aspect of "Staying Informed About Regulatory Updates." In the dynamic ecosystem of health information privacy and security, knowledge is power. The ability to stay informed and up-to-date on regulatory changes is not just a best practice, it's a necessity for maintaining HIPAA compliance. This section emphasizes the importance of keeping one's finger on the pulse of regulatory shifts and provides guidance on how to accomplish this effectively.

The Importance of Regulatory Awareness

Being informed about regulatory updates is akin to staying abreast of the weather conditions when you're navigating a ship. The sea of regulations is perpetually changing, and failing to stay informed can lead to non-compliance, resulting in heavy fines, reputational damage, and potential loss of patient trust.

Regulatory updates may introduce new requirements, modify existing ones, or even eliminate outdated provisions. By staying informed, an organization can ensure that its policies and procedures are always in line with the latest regulatory requirements.

Strategies for Staying Informed

Numerous strategies can help an organization stay informed about regulatory updates. Subscribing to relevant newsletters, participating in professional forums, attending industry conferences, and following regulatory bodies on social media are all viable strategies. For example, the HHS Office for Civil Rights, responsible for enforcing HIPAA, regularly publishes updates and guidance on its website and through various communications.

Another strategy is to leverage legal and consulting services specializing in healthcare regulations. These professionals can provide insights into how regulatory changes might impact an organization and can offer advice on necessary adaptations.

Implementing Regulatory Updates

Being informed about regulatory updates is only half the battle. The other half is effectively implementing these changes within the organization. This involves reviewing and updating the organization's policies and procedures in light of the new regulations, training staff on any new requirements, and possibly even modifying technical systems to ensure compliance.

Staying informed about regulatory updates and effectively implementing them is a continuous task, requiring commitment and resources. However, the investment is well worth it. By staying ahead of regulatory changes, an organization can ensure its compliance posture is always strong, reducing risk and fostering trust among its patients.

Building a culture of compliance

In this section, we turn our attention to a crucial aspect of any successful compliance program: "Building a Culture of Compliance." The ethos of an organization significantly influences its conduct, and a strong culture of compliance can act as the bedrock upon which effective HIPAA adherence is built.

Understanding the Culture of Compliance

A culture of compliance refers to an environment where adhering to regulations and ethical standards is ingrained in the organization's ethos. In such an environment, employees understand the importance of compliance and are actively engaged in maintaining it. Compliance is seen not as a burden, but as an integral part of the organization's operations and reputation.

Benefits of a Culture of Compliance

A strong culture of compliance can bring numerous benefits. These include improved adherence to regulations, reduced risk of violations, and increased trust from patients and partners. Moreover, when employees are invested in compliance, they are more likely to identify and report potential issues, enabling proactive risk management.

Cultivating a Culture of Compliance

Building a culture of compliance doesn't happen overnight. It requires a clear vision, ongoing commitment from all levels of the organization, and strategies tailored to the organization's unique needs and challenges. Here are some key steps towards cultivating a culture of compliance:

Leadership Commitment: The commitment to compliance must start at the top. Leaders should set the tone by demonstrating an understanding of HIPAA requirements and a commitment to meeting them. This can be done through regular communication about the importance of compliance, involvement in compliance activities, and leading by example.

Education and Training: Regular, comprehensive training is a must. Employees should understand not only the "what" of HIPAA regulations, but also the "why." They should also be trained on how to identify potential compliance issues and what to do when they encounter them.

Open Communication: Encourage open dialogue about compliance. Employees should feel comfortable raising concerns or asking questions without fear of retaliation.

Recognition and Reward: Recognize and reward employees who demonstrate a commitment to compliance. This could be through formal recognition programs, or simply through positive feedback.

Continuous Improvement: Compliance is not a one-time effort, but an ongoing process. Regularly review and update compliance strategies and initiatives, and engage employees in this process.

In the journey towards HIPAA compliance, a strong culture of compliance is a powerful ally. It can help navigate regulatory changes, mitigate risks, and ensure that the organization's commitment to protecting patient privacy is not just a regulatory requirement, but a core part of its identity.

12

Conclusion

The importance of HIPAA compliance for healthcare organizations

We have now come full circle in our exploration of HIPAA and its ramifications for the healthcare industry. Now is the time to highlight the bedrock of this entire discourse: "The Importance of HIPAA Compliance for Healthcare Organizations."

The Significance of Compliance

HIPAA compliance is not just a legal obligation for healthcare organizations. It is a fundamental aspect of patient care and trust, integral to the operations of healthcare providers, insurance companies, and any entity dealing with protected health information (PHI). Non-compliance can lead to penalties, damaged reputations, and, most importantly, breaches that put patient data at risk.

Protecting Patient Privacy

In a world where data breaches and identity theft are increasingly common, HIPAA compliance plays a critical role in preserving the privacy and security of patient data. The provisions of HIPAA ensure that every step, from data collection to storage and transmission, is carried out with stringent security measures. This commitment to privacy builds patient trust, an essential factor in the caregiver-patient relationship.

Avoiding Financial Consequences

The financial implications of non-compliance can be severe. Penalties for HIPAA violations can range from $100 to $1.5 million per violation category, per year, depending on the violation's nature and extent. Besides, the cost of a data breach can be astronomical when considering the associated expenses like notification costs, patient monitoring, regulatory fines, and potential lawsuits.

Enhancing Operational Efficiency

HIPAA compliance leads to streamlined operations. Through the establishment of defined procedures and protocols, organizations can improve their efficiency, ensure the integrity of their data, and create a more secure environment. Compliance also enables interoperability, facilitating the smooth exchange of health information and promoting better collaboration within the healthcare ecosystem.

Staying Ahead of Technological Advances

The digital age has revolutionized healthcare delivery, from telemedicine to AI diagnostics, opening new avenues for efficiency and patient care. However, it also presents new risks for patient data. Staying HIPAA compliant ensures that healthcare organizations are prepared to adapt to these changes securely, protecting patient data in the face of ever-evolving technology.

HIPAA compliance is not a destination but a continuous journey. With regulatory landscapes shifting and technological advancements rapidly changing the face of healthcare, organizations must stay vigilant, proactive, and adaptable in their compliance efforts. As we draw to a close, remember, HIPAA compliance is not just about adhering to a set of regulations - it's about upholding the trust that patients place in healthcare organizations, protecting their sensitive information, and thereby contributing to a safer, more secure healthcare environment.

Balancing privacy and security with patient care and innovation

In the dynamic healthcare landscape, one element remains at the forefront - the need to harmoniously merge the principles of privacy and security with patient care and innovation. This delicate dance forms the crux of our concluding discourse: "Balancing Privacy and Security with Patient Care and Innovation."

The Interplay of Privacy, Security, and Patient Care

HIPAA mandates the protection of patient data, ensuring privacy and security. However, these regulations are not meant to impede patient care; rather, they aim to enhance it. By safeguarding patient data, HIPAA fosters an environment of trust, where patients feel comfortable sharing sensitive health information. This openness, in turn, can lead to more accurate diagnoses, personalized treatment plans, and overall improved health outcomes.

Privacy and security also intersect with patient care in the realm of patient rights. HIPAA affords patients the right to access and control their health information. This empowerment can lead to more engaged patients, who actively participate in their healthcare, leading to better patient satisfaction and outcomes.

Innovation: A Double-Edged Sword

Innovation is undoubtedly revolutionizing healthcare. From artificial intelligence in diagnostics to telemedicine for remote care, technological advancements are streamlining healthcare delivery, improving patient access, and making healthcare more personalized and efficient.

However, each technological leap also brings with it new challenges for privacy and security. As more data is collected and shared digitally, the risk of breaches increases. Furthermore, technologies like AI and machine learning depend on vast amounts of data for accuracy, creating a potential conflict with privacy principles.

Striking the Balance

So, how can healthcare organizations strike a balance? The key is to view HIPAA not as a barrier but as a guide. Regulations should inform the way innovations are implemented, with a proactive approach to privacy and security. Here are some strategies to consider:

Data Minimization: Collect and use only the data necessary for the purpose at hand. This principle is especially relevant for AI and machine learning applications, where there might be a temptation to collect more data "just in case."

Privacy by Design: Integrate privacy and security considerations into the design phase of any new technology or process. This proactive approach can help prevent privacy and security issues from arising later on.

Regular Risk Assessments: As technology evolves, so do the potential threats. Regular risk assessments can help organizations stay ahead of new vulnerabilities and ensure they are adequately protected.

Patient Involvement: Include patients in the conversation. Educate patients about how their data is used and secured and offer them control where possible. This transparency can build trust and engagement.

Balancing privacy and security with patient care and innovation is a complex task, requiring continuous vigilance and adaptability. However, the potential rewards - from improved patient care to cutting-edge treatments - make this endeavor worthwhile. As healthcare continues to evolve, organizations that can navigate this balance will be well-positioned for success.

The ongoing responsibility of maintaining compliance

The journey through the labyrinth of HIPAA is not one that ends with the last page of this book. It is instead a perpetual endeavor, a commitment to the ongoing responsibility of maintaining compliance. The concluding section of our final chapter, "The Ongoing Responsibility of Maintaining Compliance," captures this enduring spirit of accountability.

The Constancy of Compliance

HIPAA compliance is not a one-time accomplishment, a box to be checked off and then forgotten. Instead, it is a continuous responsibility, requiring ongoing vigilance, agility, and commitment from healthcare organizations. The dynamism of the healthcare landscape, marked by evolving technologies and shifting regulatory landscapes, necessitates this perpetual attention.

Compliance is a living, breathing entity within an organization. It requires nurturing through regular risk assessments, policy reviews, and employee training. It demands responsiveness to correct any identified deficiencies and adapt to new regulations or guidance. And it requires a proactive approach to anticipate and prepare for future changes.

The Power of Commitment

The task, while challenging, is not insurmountable. The key to successful, ongoing compliance lies in the mindset. Viewing HIPAA not as a burden, but as an essential component of quality patient care, can transform the approach to compliance.

Embracing HIPAA as part of the organization's culture can turn compliance from an obligation into a mission. This shift in perspective can inspire employees at all levels to take ownership of compliance, making it a collective, organization-wide effort. A culture of compliance is self-perpetuating. It fosters an environment of openness, where employees feel comfortable raising concerns, and mistakes are viewed as opportunities for improvement rather than failures.

The Authoritative Voice

As the author of this book and a seasoned professional in the field, I urge you to embrace this ongoing responsibility with an open mind and unwavering dedication. The path to compliance may not always be straightforward, but the rewards are undeniable. Robust compliance not only safeguards against penalties but also enhances patient trust, improves operational efficiency, and paves the way for innovation.

Remember, the quest for compliance is not a solitary one. I stand with you on this journey, offering the knowledge and insights gathered through personal experience. Lean on this book as your guide, revisit it as often as needed, and always keep learning and adapting.

Your partner in compliance, Wilder...

www.ingramcontent.com/pod-product-compliance
Lightning Source LLC
La Vergne TN
LVHW051644050326
832903LV00022B/875